First published 2000 by Aurum Press Limited,
25 Bedford Avenue, London WC1B 3AT
Compilation copyright © 2000 Michelle Lovric

A catalogue record for this book is available from the British Library.

ISBN: 1-85410-734-8

Editorial assistant: Kristina Blagojevitch
Designed by Michelle Lovric and Lisa Pentreath

Printed and bound in Italy by LEGO SpA

The editor gratefully acknowledges the assistance of the following people: Judith Grant, Iain Campbell, David Franks and Lynne Curran.

ILLUSTRATION ACKNOWLEDGEMENTS:

Front cover and page 38, detail from La Dame à la Licorne: "L'Ouïe"; page 9, detail from La Dame à la Licorne: "Le Gout", both courtesy of the musée du Moyen-Age — Cluny, copyright © Photo RMN — R. G. Ojeda; Endpapers, detail from La Vie Seigneuriale: "La Lecture", courtesy of the musée du Moyen-Age — Cluny, copyright © Photo RMN — G. Blot/C. Jean.
Pages 3 and 22, Poodle on a red velvet cushion, Italian school, 18th century; page 23, A Portrait of a Young Girl holding her Pet Dog, Nathaniel Hone, both courtesy of Raphael Valls Ltd, London.
Pages 2—3, Head study of a Pointer, William Henry Hamilton Trood; page 12, Two greyhounds, Charles Emmanuel Jadin; page 24, Dante and his dog, Sir James Dromgole Linton; page 34, A white and black spotted dog with a miniature spaniel, Neapolitan school, 1671; pages 36—37, A Great Dane on the Beach, Pierre Franc Lamy, all courtesy of Sotheby's Picture Library, London.
Page 6, detail of the Satirical Papyrus, copyright © The British Museum.
Page 7, Earthenware Watch Dog, Chinese, 1st century AD; pages 30—31, Tapestry of the Pursuit of Fidelity, Alsace, 1475—1500, both courtesy of The Burrell Collection, copyright © Glasgow Museums & Art Galleries.
Victorian scraps reproduced courtesy of Mamelok Press Limited, Bury St Edmunds, England.

Dogs

The best thing about
man is the dog

Dormont de Belloy (Pierre Laurent Buyrette)
(1727—75)
French playwright

ontents

Qui me amat, amet et canem meum.
Who loves me will love my dog also.

Saint Bernard (1091—1153)

a little Book of Dogs

Michelle Lovric

AURUM PRESS

ntroduction

It is thought that the first feeding of a wild jackal by a primitive man took place 50,000 years ago. The first dog probably moved into a human dwelling as a permanent inmate some 30,000 years later. From that moment on, dogs have been seen as the natural companions of men. They have become our guards and helpers, placing the whole range of their superior instincts at our disposal, without any personal ambition except to serve. This makes them happy, insofar as we understand dog happiness. Happy, busy dogs are portrayed in the earliest art, and ancient literature. But there is more to dogs than this; they are also friends, as George Eliot points out, come to fill up the void created by human failings, and such perfect friends, being incapable of criticism, envy, dissimulation or malice.

Of course, most poems and prose about dogs are really about men and women as well. Dogs, with their saintly eyes and eager hearts, have become symbols of fidelity unto the death, and even beyond. In tomb monuments, dogs were placed at the feet of married women to indicate the faithful affection they had given and inspired during their lives. Crusaders, too, were buried with dogs at the feet of their sculpted likenesses: this signified that the soldier had followed the standard of Christ as faithfully as a dog would follow his master.

Nor are dogs mere machines of life and love. They seem to offer an insight into higher spiritual values. When Odysseus returned from his years in the wilderness, it was only his adoring dog Argos who recognized him.

In many other great legends, the hero — be it King Arthur, Cuchulain or Fingal — is always accompanied by his hound. In Christian writings, dogs have been associated with Saint Roch, the patron of plague, and also Saints Bernard, Benignus and Wendolin. Reputed to be able to heal wounds by licking them, dogs were seen as metaphors for the priests who cured the spiritual wounds of their flocks. Black and white dogs were particularly seen as the emblems of the Dominican fathers. Saint Dominic's symbol is a dog with a flaming torch in his mouth.

History is full of famous dogs, some made so by the devotion of their eloquent owners: Elizabeth Barrett Browning's Flush, Queen Victoria's Dash, William Wordsworth's Music, for example. Other dogs, such as Greyfriar's Bobby, who watched over his master's grave for 20 years, have surpassed their owners' fame with acts of fidelity, heroism and sagacity. Such tales are too numerous for us to include more than a very few examples in this anthology. To distil the nature of dogs, and convey some of the pleasure they give, we also include short extracts from writers such as Dorothy Parker, Colette and Robert Louis Stevenson, who have all taken dogs as their theme to illustrate points about human, as well as animal, nature.

Dog lovers are quick to point out the wholehearted humour of the dog, and the emotional refuge he offers with his unqualified love and approval. We envy his uncomplicated love life, and his unrestrained enthusiasm for simple joys. Dogs provide us with an opportunity to display unconditional love as well as receive it. The artist Vere Temple once described a dog as a necessary emotional safety valve in a family. However, there is pain in store for anyone who loves a dog. Rudyard Kipling warned: "Beware of giving your heart to a dog to tear", for dogs' lives among us are sadly but inevitably shorter than our own.

Dog Lore

While all other Creatures are in a State of Enmity with us, some flying into Woods and Wildernesses to escape our Tyranny ... Dogs alone enter into voluntary Friendship with us

... If we look back into ancient History, we shall find the wisest and most celebrated Nations of Antiquity, as it were, contending with one another, which should pay the greatest Honour to Dogs. The old Astronomers denominated Stars after their Name ...

Francis Coventry (?—1759)
English satirical writer and divine

It was about 8000 years ago that dog and man first started going together. They started out as business partners. They hunted together.

James R. Kinney
20th-century American vet and writer

Through association with a dog, man doubled his perceptions.

John Steinbeck (1902—68)
American novelist

And first of the animals which have had more influence over the human soul, in its modern life, than ever Apis or the crocodile had over Egyptian — the dog ... Venetians always introduced the dog as a contrast to the high aspects of humanity. They do this, not because they consider him the basest of animals, but the highest — the connecting link between man and animals.

John Ruskin (1819—1900)
English writer, artist, designer and philosopher

DOG SUPERSTITIONS

BAD LUCK

Meeting a barking dog at dawn or a black dog crossing in front of you.

A dog running between a pair of lovers: they will quarrel.

A dog running between a woman's legs: she will be punished by her husband or father.

GOOD LUCK

A greyhound with a white spot on its forehead; meeting a white dog in the morning, or three white dogs together; a black dog following you home.

To see the image of a black dog in the fire: a friend is near.

Meeting a black and white dog on the way to a business deal: it will go well.

An unknown dog entering your house: a new friendship.

DOG DREAMS

Dreaming of a black dog: a friend is near.

Dreaming of dogs in general: matters of instinct and conscience are to the fore. It can also mean fear of rejection on the grounds of unattractiveness.

Dreaming of a vicious dog: envy and unscrupulousness.

DOG REMEDIES

Against rheumatism: melted dog fat.

Against scrofula: a dried dog's tongue worn around neck.

Against skin sores: the lick of a dog.

Against jaundice: a poultice of dog's head and wine.

DOG DEATH OMENS

A dog howling outside at night or howling once and then falling silent.

A dog howling persistently in front of a house where someone lies ill.

A dog digging a hole in your garden.

The fact that a dog tied up to a sick belly cures it inside means that the words of our Lord purify the secrets of men's hearts ... And when a dog, out of greed, lets fall in to the water what he held in his mouth to grasp the reflection he sees in the water, he is like those ignorant and foolish people who out of greed seek what they do not know and lose what is theirs. So they cannot get what they lust for and lose forever what they dropped for nothing.

Pierre de Beauvais
13th-century French writer

Doggerel

A dog is brave at his own door.

Behar proverb

Let Hercules himself do what he may, The cat will mew, the dog will have his day.

William Shakespeare (1564—1616)
English poet and playwright

Who sleepeth with dogs shall rise with fleas.

John Florio (c. 1533—1625)
English teacher
and translator

His bark is worse than his bite.

George Herbert (1593—1633)
English poet

Rejoice in the sea but stay on the land,
Rejoice in the mountains but stay in the valley,
Rejoice in the cat but stroke the dog.

Venetian proverb

A dog starved at his master's gate Predicts the ruin of the state.

William Blake (1757—1827)
English poet, painter
and mystic

🐕 **Dog in a manger:** one who would prevent another from enjoying what he himself does not want. It alludes to the fable of the dog who sat in the manger and would not allow the oxen to eat the hay, although he would not touch it himself. 🐕 **The dogs have not dined:** a common saying to any one whose shirt hangs out behind. 🐕 **To blush like a blue dog:** i.e. not at all. 🐕 **Dog in a doublet:** a daring, resolute fellow. 🐕 **Dog's portion:** a lick and a smell. 🐕 **Dog's rig:** to copulate till you are tired, and then turn tail to it. 🐕 **Dog's soup:** rain water. 🐕 **A black dog has walked over him:** a sullen person. The Devil is thought to take the form of a black dog sometimes. The Romans considered a black dog with its pups an unlucky omen. 🐕 **A dog's chance:** virtually no chance at all.

THE CALUMNIATED DOG

Can anybody tell me why the dog has been selected by the universal voice of mankind to embody everything that is opprobious? ... Now, I have reflected deeply on this pugnacious subject, and without a glimmer of satisfaction to my doubts. I ask, again, of this crowd of persecutors, why — dog? Why not cow, or ox, or horse, as well? It is my private opinion that the "dog has had his day". Let people now hit somebody of their own size.

Fanny Fern (Sarah Payson Willis) (1811—72)
American writer

The nature of dogs

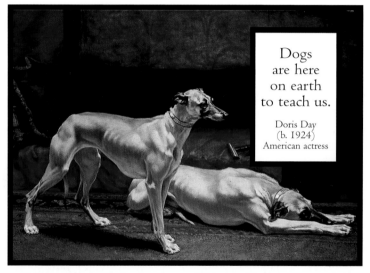

Dogs
are here
on earth
to teach us.

Doris Day
(b. 1924)
American actress

He knows to whom above him to give himself ... He knows the supreme duties which we all do not know. He has a morality which surpasses all that he is able to discover within himself ...

Maurice Maeterlinck (1862—1949)
Belgian poet and playwright

Of all carnivorous quadrupeds, the dog kind must indisputably claim the preference; being the most intelligent, courageous and domestic attendant on man.

from *Natural History*, 1823.

... And are not these dumb friends of ours persons rather than things? Is not their soul ampler, as Plato would say, than their body, and contains rather than is contained? ... And when we look each other in the face ... is it not as much the dog within looking out from his eyes — the windows of his soul — as it is the man from his?

John Brown (1810—82)
Scottish physician and essayist

The civilization, the manners and the morals of dog-kind are to a great extent subordinated to those of his ancestral master, man. This animal, in many ways so superior, has accepted a position of inferiority ...

Robert Louis Stevenson (1850—94)
Scottish writer

One of the reasons why dogs are given credit for serious thinking is the formation of their eyebrows.

Robert Benchley (1889—1945)
American writer

"Poor dog! I've a strange feeling about the dumb things, as if they wanted to speak, and it was a trouble to 'em because they couldn't. I can't help being sorry for the dogs a lump ... But they may well have more in them than they know how to make us understand, for we can't say half what we feel with all our words."

Dinah Morris speaks, in *Adam Bede* by George Eliot (1819—80)
English novelist

It is by muteness that a dog becomes for one so utterly beyond value; with him one is at peace, where words play no torturing tricks. When he just sits, loving, and knows that he is being loved, those are the moments that I think are precious to a dog.

John Galsworthy (1867—1933)
English novelist and playwright

It is one of his most charming traits that he thinks visibly.

Edward Verrall Lucas (1868—1938)
English essayist and biographer

When you talk to a dog, a soul answers you.

Bam Wildfire
19th-century American writer

Mr Lee was my first American Pekingese ... He was the rarest of the rare not because of his colour, a golden honey, but because he could talk. My friends considered his vocabulary to be somewhat limited, but they testified without prompting that he could say quite distinctly, "I want the ball" and "I love you", as well as "Up yours", and a couple of other choice bits.

Beatrice Lillie (1898—1989)
Canadian singer

are quadrupeds. That is to say,

Dogs, like horses,

they have four rupeds,

Frank Muir
(1920—88)
English writer and comedian

16

one at each corner.

Shapes & styles of dogs

A satisfactory classification of the different kinds of dog has not yet been arrived at. What some naturalists regard as types, others regard as mere mongrel races.

from *Beeton's Dictionary of Natural History*, 1871.

I like a bit of a mongrel myself, whether it's a man or a dog: they're the best for everyday.

George Bernard Shaw (1856—1950)
Irish writer

Dog owners are notoriously biased in their opinions on breeds. Nearly all of them are one-breed fanciers. They know there exist odd-looking animals walking around on four legs claiming to be dogs but in their hearts they never quite accept any breed but their own.

James R. Kinney
20th-century American vet and writer

18

In real life dogs have their own class distinctions, quite apart from those of their owners.

Cecily Boas
from *Birds and Beasts in English Literature*, 1934.

INSTRUCTIONS TO A PAINTER

Happiest of the spaniel race,
Painter, with thy colours grace;
Draw his forehead large and high,
Draw his blue and humid eye;
Draw his neck so smooth and round,
Little neck with ribands bound;
And the musely swelling breast
Where the loves and graces rest;
And the spreading even back,
Soft, and sleek, and glossy black;
And the tail that gently twines.
Like the tendrils of the vines;
And the silky twisted hair,
Shadowing thick the velvet ear;
Velvet ears, which, hanging low,
O'er the veiny temples flow ...

Jonathan Swift (1667—1745)
Irish writer

It is almost impossible to make a satisfactory drawing of a dog from the point of view of form alone — without the likeness, the drawing becomes meaningless. Dogs, like human beings, are such definite personalities that their form is secondary to their character.

Vere Temple
20th-century English writer and artist

Ay, in the catalogue ye go for men;
As hounds, and greyhounds, mongrels, spaniels, curs,
Shoughs, water-rugs and demi-wolves, are clept
All by the name of dogs: the valued file
Distinguishes the swift, the slow, the subtle,
The housekeeper, the hunter, every one
According to the gift
which bounteous nature
Hath in him closed.

William Shakespeare (1564—1616)
English poet and playwright

By cliff and chine, and hollow-nestling wood
 Thrilled with the poignant savour of the sea,
 All in the crisp light of a wintry morn,
 We walked, my friend and I, preceded still
By one whose silken and voluminous suit,
 His courtly ruff, snow-pure mid golden tan,
  His grandly feathered legs slenderly strong,
   The broad and flowing billow of his breast,
    His delicate ears and superfine long nose,
     With that last triumph, his distinguished tail,
     In their collective glory spoke his race
      The flower of Collie aristocracy.
       Yet, from his traits, how absent that reserve,
        That stillness on a base of power, which marks,
    In men and mastiffs, the selectly sprung!
   For after all, his high-life attributes,
    His trick of doing nothing with an air,
     His *salon* manners and society smile,
   Were but skin-deep, factitious, and you saw
    The bustling despot of the mountain flock,
   And pastoral dog-of-all-work, underlie
   The fashionable modern lady's pet ...

Sir William Watson (1858—1935)
English poet

A WRITER'S DOGS

My bulldogs are adorable, with faces
like toads that have been sat on.

Sidonie Gabrielle Colette (1873—1954)
French novelist

A BOY'S DOG

There is a degree of hopeless and irreclaimable vagabondage expressed
in this epithet ... it is the lowest step in the social scale to which a
respectable canine can descend ... the Boy's Dog is the thrall of an
entire juvenile community ... Serving not the individual boy so much as
the boy element and principle. In their active sports, in small thefts, raids
into back-yards, window-breaking, and other minor juvenile recreations
he is a full participant.

Francis Bret Harte (1836—1902)
American writer

A QUEEN'S DOG

I sent for Dashy, who Lord M[elbourne] accused of
having crooked legs, which I wouldn't allow! We put him
on the table and he was very much petted and admired
by Lord M, who was so funny about him! We gave him
tea and Lord M said, "I wonder if lapping is a pleasant
sensation," — for that is a thing we had never felt.

Queen Victoria (1819—1901)

Dogged Love

Whenever a man is lonely, God sends him a dog.

Alphonse Marie Louis de Lamartine (1790—1869)
French poet, historian and statesman

Where one dog lives and loves,
there at least is one friend faithful.

Ouida (Marie Louise de la Ramée) (1839—1908)
English novelist

The way Liz Taylor looks at Richard Burton.
The way Zsa Zsa looks at mink.
That's how a poodle looks at its master.

Jacqueline Susann (1926—74)
American novelist

He loved as only a dog can love — or an angel.

William J. Locke (1863—1930)
English novelist

Only my dogs will not betray me.

Maria Callas (1923—77)
Greek opera singer

My little old dog:
A heart-beat at my feet.

Edith Wharton (1861—1937)
American novelist

Dogs are my passion ...

George Eliot (Mary Ann Evans)
(1819—80) English writer

Dog, *n.* A kind of additional or subsidiary
Deity designed to catch the overflow and
surplus of the world's worship.

Ambrose Bierce (1842—1914)
American journalist and writer

I am one who turns practically faint with
love at the sight of a dog a block away ...

Dorothy Parker (1893—1967)
American journalist and writer

Dogs are old and experienced in the
practice of selling themselves ... by the
time he is six weeks old the average puppy
is already as wily and full of tricks as an
Armenian rug salesman, and considerably
more non-resistible.

James R. Kinney
20th-century American vet and writer

I loved dogs even more than I loved boys.

Marie Dressler (Leila von Koerber) (1869—1934)
Canadian actress

24

We Meet at Morn, my Dog and I
Still half in dream, upon the stair I hear
A patter coming nearer and more near,
And then upon my chamber door
A gentle tapping;
And next a scuffle on the passage floor,
And after that a cry, half sneeze, half yapping;
And then I know that "Oscar" lies to watch
Until the noiseless maid will lift the latch.
And like a spring
That gains its power by being tightly stayed
The impatient thing
Into the room
Its whole glad heart doth fling;
And ere the gloom
Melts into light and window-blinds are rolled,
I hear a leap upon the bed,
I feel a creeping towards me — a soft head,
And on my face
By way of an embrace
A tender nose and cold —
And on my hand like sun-warmed rose-leaves flung,
The least faint flicker of the gentlest tongue,
And so my dog and I have met and sworn
Fresh love and fealty for another morn.

Hardwick Drummond Rawnsley (1850—1920)
English poet

He is very imprudent, a dog is. He never makes it his business to inquire whether you are in the right or in the wrong, never bothers as to whether you are going up or down upon life's ladder, never asks whether you are rich or poor, silly or wise, sinner or saint.

Jerome K. Jerome (1859—1927)
English writer

Man is the God of the Dog.

Francis Bacon (1561—1626)
English philosopher and statesman

The plain fact that my dog loves me more than I love him is undeniable and always fills me with a certain feeling of shame. The dog is ever ready to lay down his life for me.

Konrad Z. Lorenz (1903—89)
Austrian zoologist and ethnologist

Dogs make shift with anything for love.

Enid Bagnold (1889—1981)
English novelist and playwright

Dogs are the tsars of forgiveness in this world.

Deirdre Purcell
Contemporary Irish writer

He has been known to lie days and nights on the grave of his dead master, and never more to be persuaded to taste food; but through rain and cold, light and darkness, remain there until he died. The love of father or mother could not go beyond this ...

from *The Young Angler, Naturalist, and Pigeon and Rabbit Fancier*, 1860.

He will sleep on the cold ground where the wintry winds blow and the snow drives fiercely if only he may be near his master's side. He will kiss the hand that has no food to offer. He will lick the wounds and sores that come in encounter with the roughness of the world. He guards the sleep of his pauper master as if he were a prince. When all other friends desert he remains.

George G. Vest
19th-century American senator

So much do dogs adore their owners, than one can read how, when King Garamantes was captured by his enemies and sold into slavery, two hundred of his hounds, having made up a party, rescued him from exile out of the middle of the whole battle-line of his foes, and fought those who resisted ... The hound of King Lisimachus threw itself into the flames when its master's funeral pyre had been lighted and was burnt up by the fire in company with him. In the days when Appius and Junius Pictimus were consuls, a dog which could not be driven away accompanied its master — who had been condemned into prison — and followed him howling after he had been executed. And when, from the compassion of the Roman people, food was offered to it, it carried the victuals to the mouth of the dead man. At last, when the corpse was thrown into the Tyber, it tried to hold the body up, swimming beside it.

from *The Book of Beasts, a Latin Bestiary of the Twelfth Century*, translated by T. H. White.

FLUSH OR FAUNUS

You see this dog. It was but yesterday
I mused forgetful of his presence here
Till thought on thought drew downward tear on tear,
When from the pillow where wet-cheeked I lay,
A head as hairy as Faunus thrust its way
Right sudden against my face, — two golden-clear
Great eyes astonished mine, — a drooping ear
Did flap me on either cheek to dry the spray!
I started first as some Arcadian
Amazed by goatly god in twilight grove,
But as the bearded vision closelier ran
My tears off, I knew Flush, and rose above
Surprise and sadness, — thanking the true Pan
Who, by low creatures, leads to heights of love.

Elizabeth Barrett Browning (1806—61)
English poet

Silvis aspera, blanda domi.
Fierce in the woods,
gentle at home.

Martial (Marcus Valerius Martialis)
(c. 40—104) Roman poet and epigrammatist

Hound Dog
appetites & instincts

The call of the wild — Spring running — whatever it is — that besets men and dogs, seldom attained full mastery over him; but one could often see it struggling against his devotion to the scent of us, and, watching the dumb contest, I have time and again wondered how far this civilization of ours was justifiably imposed on him; how far the love for us that we had so carefully implanted could ever replace in him the satisfaction of his primitive wild yearnings.

John Galsworthy (1867—1933)
English novelist and playwright

31

My bitch is asleep. She is sleeping the way French bulldogs sleep, which means that she is all twitches, imagined hunts, delicate convulsions of the jowls, and efforts to escape, to bark, perhaps to speak.

Sidonie Gabrielle Colette (1873—1954)
French novelist

Instinct is a poor word to use to express
what some dogs have done.

from *The Young Angler, Naturalist, and Pigeon and Rabbit Fancier*, 1860.

Of course what he most intensely dreams
of is being taken out on walks.

Henry James (1843—1916)
American novelist

Witness the depth of his concern and zeal
About minutest issues: shall we take
This path or that? — it matters not a straw —
But just a moment unresolved we stand,
And all his personality, from ears
To tip of tail, is interrogative;
And when from pure indifference we decide,
How he vociferates! how he bounds ahead!
With what enthusiasm he ratifies,
Applauds, acclaims our choice 'twixt right and left,
As though some hoary problem over which
The world had puckered immemorial brows,
Were solved at last, and all life launched anew!

Sir William Watson (1858—1935)
English poet

                    ... the dog, withheld
A moment from the vermin that he sees
Before him, shivers, ere he springs and kills.

Alfred, Lord Tennyson (1809—92)
English poet

The dog with inward yelp and restless

A dog must be
either eating, asleep
or interested.

Captain Robert Falcon Scott (1868—1912)
English explorer

foot plies his function of the woodland.

Titus Lucretius Carus (c. 99—55 BC), Roman poet and philosopher

To a neighbour who told her her dog was a female:
"I always call dogs 'he'. It don't do to notice everything."

Dorothy Parker (1893—1967)
American journalist and writer

I can't understand why people throw sticks to dogs. Dogs aren't
particularly interested in sticks, what they are interested in is crotches.

Jenny Eclair
Contemporary English comedienne

When asked by a young person what two dogs were doing, the English actor Noël Coward (1899—1973) explained: "Well, the one in front is blind, and the other one is kindly pushing her to St Dunstan's Home for the Blind."

It is an animal whose dominant sense is that of smell and one which has no horror of excrement, and that is not ashamed of its sexual functions.

Sigmund Freud (1856—1939)
Austrian neurologist and founder of psychoanalysis

With all his development and for all his fine civilized airs, the dog's attitude towards love remains today exactly the same as it was in 8000 BC. He still considers love simple. He still insists that love is a matter of physical attraction, gratification, no time lost in between, and with no fond lingering notions afterwards and no remorse.

James R. Kinney
20th-century American vet and writer

making the dog laugh

I think every family should have a dog:
it is like having a perpetual baby: it is the
plaything and crony of the whole house.

John Brown (1810—82)
Scottish physician and essayist

Enjoying better spirits and not crushed under
material care, he is far more theatrical than the
average man. His whole life, if he be a dog of any
pretension to gallantry, is spent in a vain show, and
in the hot pursuit of admiration.

Robert Louis Stevenson (1850—94)
Scottish writer

The great pleasure of a dog is that you may make
a fool of yourself with him and not only will he
not scold you, but he will make a fool of himself too.

Samuel Butler (1835—1902)
English writer, painter and musician

H pleasurable and excited state of mind, associated with affection, is exhibited by some dogs in a very peculiar manner, namely by grinning.

Charles Darwin (1809—82)
English naturalist

I believe that if a dog could speak as we often wish, he would express himself crudely, using rough and vulgar expressions ... He is a good-hearted fellow, but he is not a gentleman.

Karel Čapek (1890—1938)
Czech journalist and writer

Dog heaven

Do they know, as we do that their time must come?
Yes, they know, at rare moments.

John Galsworthy (1867—1933)
English novelist and playwright

When God created the world, He evidently did not foresee the future bond of friendship between man and the dog, or perhaps He had definite and, to us, inexplicable reasons for assigning to the dog a span of life five times shorter than that of his master.

Konrad Z. Lorenz (1903—89)
Austrian zoologist and ethnologist

As I was wont to straggle out
To your house, oh! how glad the dog,
With low-put nose, would nimbly jog,
Along my path and hunt about;
And his great pleasure was to run
By timber'd hedge and banky ledge,
And ended where my own begun,
At your old door and stonen floor.

And there, as time was gliding by,
With me so quick, with him so slow,
How he would look at me, and blow,
From time to time, a whining sigh,
That meant, "Now come along the land,
With timber'd knolls, and rabbit holes,
I can't think what you have on hand,
With this young face, in this old place."

William Barnes (1801—86)
English poet

The death of a dog is the end of an era.

Laura Chester (b. 1949)
American writer

WHEN OLD JACK DIED

When Old Jack died, we stayed from school (they said,
At home, we needn't go that day), and none
Of us ate any breakfast — only one,
And that was Papa — and his eyes were red
When he came round where we were, by the shed
Where Jack was lying, half-way in the sun
And half-way in the shade. When we begun
To cry out loud, Pa turned and dropped his head
And went away; and Mamma, she went back
Into the kitchen. Then, for a long while,
All to ourselves, like, we stood there and cried ...

When Old Jack died, it seemed to us, some way,
That all the other dogs in town were pained
With our bereavement, and some that were chained,
Even, unslipped their collars on that day
To visit Jack in state, as though to pay
A last, sad tribute there, while neighbours craned
Their heads above the high board fence, and deigned
To sigh "Poor Dog!" remembering how they
Had cuffed him, when alive, perchance, because,
For love of them he leaped to lick their hands —
Now, that he could not, were they satisfied?
We children thought that, as we crossed his paws,
And o'er his grave, 'way down the bottom-lands,
Wrote "Our First Love Lies Here," when Old Jack died.

James Whitcomb Riley (1849—1916)
American poet

Both man and woman wept when thou wert dead;
Not only for a thousand thoughts that were,
Old household thoughts, in which thou hadst thy share;
But for some precious boons vouchsafed to thee,
Found scarcely any where in like degree!
For love, that comes wherever life and sense
Are given by God, in thee was most intense ...
Hence if we wept, it was not done in shame;
Our tears from passion and from reason came,
And, therefore, shalt thou be an honoured name!

William Wordsworth (1770—1850)
English poet

41

And is this all that is left of you —
One little grave and a pang to us?

William Hurrell Mallock (1849—1923)
English poet

Do, when the love that
lights up in your eyes goes out,
It will come back to life somehow,
somewhere in heaven.

Alphonse Marie Louis de Lamartine (1790—1869)
French poet, historian and statesman